T... FUNNIEST CELTIC QUOTES... EVER!

Also available

The Funniest Rangers Quotes... Ever!

The Funniest Scotland Quotes... Ever!

The Funniest Arsenal Quotes... Ever!

The Funniest Liverpool Quotes... Ever!

The Funniest Chelsea Quotes... Ever!

The Funniest West Ham Quotes... Ever!

The Funniest Spurs Quotes... Ever!

The Funniest Man City Quotes... Ever!

The Funniest Newcastle Quotes... Ever!

The Funniest United Quotes... Ever!

The Funniest Leeds Quotes... Ever!

The Funniest Boro Quotes... Ever!

The Funniest Forest Quotes... Ever!

The Funniest Sunderland Quotes... Ever!

The Funniest Leicester Quotes... Ever!

The Funniest Saints Quotes... Ever!

The Funniest Everton Quotes... Ever!

The Funniest Villa Quotes... Ever!

The Funniest Ireland Quotes... Ever!

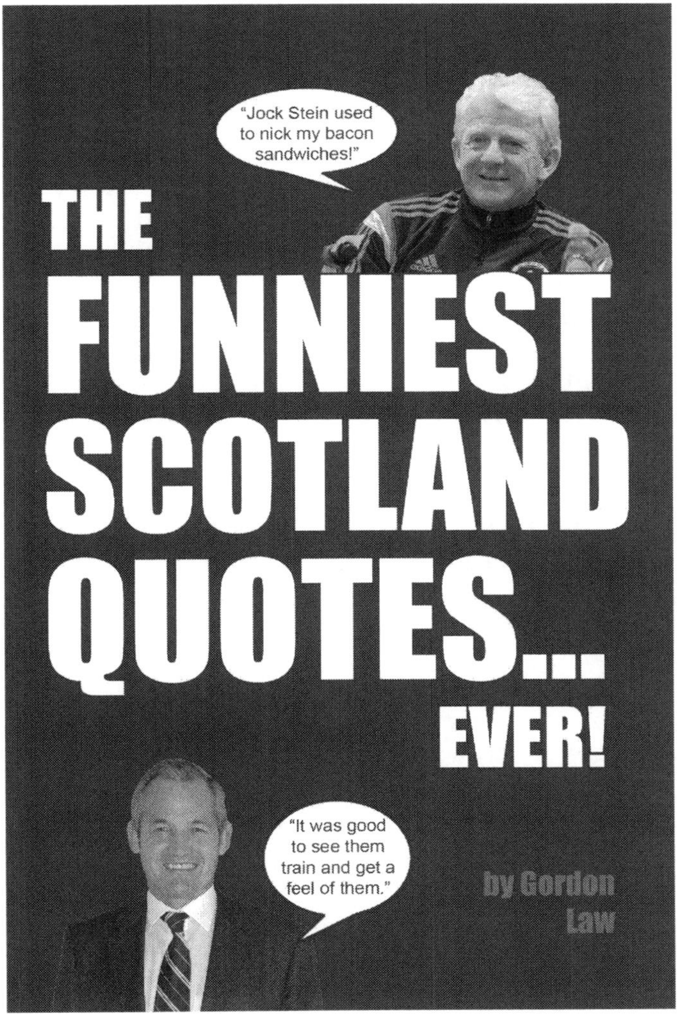
"Jock Stein used to nick my bacon sandwiches!"
THE FUNNIEST SCOTLAND QUOTES... EVER!
"It was good to see them train and get a feel of them."
by Gordon Law

Printed in Europe and the USA

ISBN: 9781729463468
Imprint: Independently published

Photos courtesy of: Influential Photography/Shutterstock.com; Tomasz Bidermann/Shutterstock.com.

Contents

Introduction

There are many inspirational quotes from the great Celtic manager Jock Stein that adorn the walls of the club's stadium.

The words of Stein, who led the Bhoys to nine straight league titles and a famous European Cup triumph, act as a reminder of the legendary figure.

He was not only immensely successful but was also an incredibly charismatic figure who produced more than his fair share of witty remarks during his Celtic Park reign.

Fellow Scot Gordon Strachan was another manager who used to come out with funny sound bites – from harsh statements to bad jokes – and journalists were often the ones to bear the brunt of a verbal lashing.

Strachan's post-match press conferences were always entertaining as he loved to give an answer laced with sarcasm or blast a reporter for asking a daft question.

There have been cringeworthy comments from Brendan Rodgers over the years, pearls of wisdom from Martin O'Neill, while Neil Lennon was never one to mince his words.

Celtic players have also provided us with hilarious moments, from Artur Boruc to Chris Sutton, while Frank McAvennie's off-field antics have been a source of amusement.

Many of their classic quips can be found in this unique collection and I hope you laugh as much reading this book as I did in compiling it.

Gordon Law

THE FUNNIEST CELTIC QUOTES... EVER!

CALL THE MANAGER

"If you get a lot of chances and miss them then there is nothing you can do. It's human error. There's no way I can come in at the end of the game and stick bamboo shoots up the fingernails for missing chances."

Gordon Strachan after a goalless draw in a season opener against Kilmarnock

"Do you see that big f*cking moat that surrounds the park? It's going straight in there."

Bertie Auld to Tommy Gemmell who was shaping up for a free-kick in the closing stages of the European Cup Final

"They have six players from Argentina in their team, so that means a riot for a start."

Jock Stein on facing Atletico Madrid in the 1974 European Cup semi-final

"It was orgasmic, if I can say that. Maybe even better than that!"

Ronny Deila after a late winner against Aberdeen

"I never see anything, I'm like the fourth official, I never see anything at any time."

Gordon Strachan after a fan went onto the pitch against AC Milan

"It's good to see Shaun [Maloney] and John [Kennedy] back training. It's fantastic they both got back on the same week because it means they don't have to split up at any time whatsoever. Now they're called the Twins, after the film with Danny DeVito and Arnold Schwarzenegger."

Gordon Strachan is happy his duo are back fit again

"An agent said to me once that you have to blindfold a player and gag them to get them up here – then put a big wad in their pocket. So it's definitely not easy."

Gordon Strachan on the challenges of getting players to move north of the border

"I didn't speak to the referee afterwards on the pitch. It wasn't the time or place. But I'll definitely speak to him if he lets the lock off his door."
Brendan Rodgers blasts the referee for a penalty decision against Ross County

"You are really going mental when you are having arguments with people who are not even here."
Gordon Strachan on rumours he had a tiff with Paul Telfer who had left a month earlier

"When we were going to put Roy [Keane] on he disappeared to the toilet."
Gordon Strachan couldn't find his sub

"Maybe I scored a goal against his favourite team 30 years ago."
Gordon Strachan on referee Stuart Dougal who sent him to the stands

"Lots of young players these days look good, they smell nice, but they don't put the work in."
Brendan Rodgers on youngsters making the first team

"I have thought the SFA was like that since I was four years old because my granny told me."
Peter Grant fumes at the SFA's delayed registration of new signing Jorge Cadette

"It hasn't just happened overnight."

Brendan Rodgers states the obvious after Celtic broke the club's own British record of 62 games undefeated

"It's just the ramblings of someone who has failed as a coach. I don't take too much notice of Bernd Schuster."

Neil Lennon blasts the ex-Real Madrid boss who criticised Celtic's style of football

"Paul told me that's the first one he's missed, which I find very surprising having seen that."

Gordon Strachan on Paul Hartley's penalty against Hearts

"When they scored their third I actually thought they'd gone off into Seville to celebrate."

Martin O'Neill on Porto's time-wasting while celebrating their goals

"At Falkirk the other week, the police were asked to speak to me about smiling at the crowd. Someone reported me for smiling in his direction. Obviously it's not the best smile in the world. I can see a lot better smiles, but I never knew my smile could be offensive, but there you go. That's the world we live in just now."

Gordon Strachan on a complaint from a supporter

"We climbed three mountains and then proceeded to throw ourselves off them."
Billy McNeill after a 5-4 European Cup Winners' Cup victory over Partizan Belgrade, but Celtic went out on away goals with the score 6-6 on aggregate

Reporter: "Gordon, tell us how you're feeling winning back-to-back titles here today."
Gordon Strachan: "Sorry I cannot describe my position to anybody... I'd love to but.... I've never taken drugs but I wonder if it's a bit like this!"
Gordon Strachan on clinching the title after a stoppage-time winner against Kilmarnock

"When I'm dead, it will be inscribed on my headstone: 'This isn't as bad as that night in Bratislava'."

Gordon Strachan after a 5-0 Champions League defeat by Slovakian club Artmedia Bratislava

"If I have been sent off for looking like a strange wee man, then I can't appeal against that. If he has sent me to the stand because I'm only 5ft 5in, then I can't argue with that... but until I find out what he sent me to the stand for, then it has to be a problem."

Gordon Strachan is baffled as to why he was sent from the dugout against Hearts

"The transfer list thing went out in the 1970s, it doesn't happen here so it's a mysterious one. I was having a cup of tea and a rhubarb tart when I saw it and I nearly spluttered."

Gordon Strachan on speculation that Kenny Miller had been transfer listed

"I don't know what you mean... what do you want us to do? We played five at the back, do you want me to play seven along the back, one midfielder, one goalkeeper and a striker?"

An exasperated Brendan Rodgers loses count of his players after a 7-1 defeat against Paris Saint-Germain

"We don't consider we lost on football, but to a circus turn."

Jock Stein doesn't believe penalties should decide a game after Celtic's shoot-out loss to Inter in the European Cup semi-final

"If he did jump into the crowd, then the referee had to book him. I can't tell the players before a game that, if they score, they shouldn't jump into the crowd. If my hip was a bit better, I'd have been in there as well."

Gordon Strachan after Jan Vennegoor of Hesselink's stoppage-time winner against Inverness earned him a second yellow card

Inter Milan: "We will pay Celtic £100,000 if you will let us have your right winger Jimmy Johnstone."

Jock Stein: "For which match?"

"If the players are looking for a sign from me, I'm sorry but I'll be in the toilet somewhere."

Martin O'Neill ahead of the UEFA Cup Final against Porto

"Angels don't win you anything except a place in heaven. Football teams need one or two vagabonds."

Billy McNeill on the ideal make-up of a team

"It was John [Barnes] who signed all the players at Celtic. I don't know who was the worst although there were more bad ones than good ones."

Kenny Dalglish passes the buck

"The word I said to them was 'infrangible'. That was the word I wrote up on the paper. Stuart Armstrong understood it but I did actually say, 'For those of you who don't understand I wrote the meaning below'. So 'to be unbroken', that is another word for their vocabulary."

Brendan Rodgers after his unbeaten Celtic side won the title

"There is as much chance as Frank McAvennie leaving Celtic as there is of us losing 5-1 tomorrow."

Bill McNeill the day before Celtic lost 5-1 to Rangers – and just months later McAvennie ended up departing the club

"I've seen [Shunsuke] Nakamura and had a laugh about it. I peek round the corner when he's doing his weights and sing 'Cheerio, Cheerio'."

Gordon Strachan on reports that the midfielder is being lured away

"It's dangerous to try and fight him [Alex Ferguson] when you've got a sponge and he's armed with a machine gun."

Gordon Strachan on the great manager

"I just felt that the whole night, the conditions and taking everything into consideration and everything being equal, and everything is equal, we should have got something from the game, but we didn't."

John Barnes on equality in football

"Neil Lennon wasn't sent off for scoring a goal, and that's what annoys me."

Martin O'Neill wants reds for the right reasons

"When I die you can put on my tombstone, 'Andy Goram broke his heart'."

Tommy Burns on the Rangers keeper who has thwarted Celtic many times

"We are very lucky, we have got no d*ckheads."

Brendan Rodgers hails his Celtic team after they recovered from defeat at Hearts with wins over Partick Thistle and Aberdeen

"Have the first issue ready for the week after the Scottish Cup Final and leave a blank space on page one for a picture of the boys with the Cup."

Jock Stein on the new magazine Celtic View

"Jock Stein would pour Coca-Cola down the sink if young players were drinking it – it was too gassy."

Lou Macari

"When they attacked we were four players down."

Tommy Burns on fielding Andy Thom, Paolo di Canio, Pierre van Hooijdonk and Jorge Cadette in a UEFA Cup loss

Journalist: "What qualities will Jan Vennegoor of Hesselink bring?"

Gordon Strachan: "I have no idea, but I said I'd bring a big name to the club."

"One of my jobs is to find out why we spent so much of our money on Rafael Scheidt."

Martin O'Neill on the £5m signing made by John Barnes

"I much prefer watching videos, it is not necessary to go and see a player."

John Barnes after he bought Scheidt

"24's on. Jack Bauer, he's some man. Wouldn't mind him in the back four!"

Gordon Strachan when asked what he's doing that night to celebrate Celtic's 2006 title success

"I just went along to see him, to see how many times he was caught offside – and he didn't let me down."

Gordon Strachan on why he watched Norwich's friendly against Falkirk – it wasn't to sign Darren Huckerby

Reporter: "So, Gordon, in what areas were Motherwell better than you today?"

Gordon Strachan: "Mainly that big green one out there."

The Celtic manager after a 1-0 home defeat against the Well

"I wouldn't put my house on it. I've worked too hard for 35 years to risk that."

Gordon Strachan when asked if Cetic can win 2-0 at Barcelona

"I don't want to mix up one game with another. When you go to the market, apples are apples and plums are plums."

Jozef Venglos

"There's a lot of ice in that dressing room – it's like the dining room on the Titanic in there."

Gordon Strachan after a rough-and-tumble game at Hearts

THE FUNNIEST CELTIC QUOTES... EVER!

BOARDROOM BANTER

"It seemed to me Fergus [McCann] had no respect for football people, suggesting they were too emotional and of low IQ."

Tommy Burns has a pop at Celtic's owner

"I like any moment when we've had victories at Celtic Park – especially over teams wearing blue."

Celtic majority shareholder Dermot Desmond takes a swipe at Rangers

"He is the finest man I have ever met in my life. That's quite an accolade."

General manager Jock Brown on Jozef Venglos and a hard man to please

"By the time June 30 comes around, a lot of the players are going to be reminded of the Dionne Warwick song, 'Do You Know the Way to San Jose?'. That's the one with the line about 'All the stars that never were are parking cars and pumping gas'."

Fergus McCann's analogy about Celtic's four out-of-contract players

"Before a Rangers game, chairman Bob Kelly came into the dressing room to say a few words and talked about sporting behaviour. When he left, Big Jock closed the door and said, 'For a start, you can forget all that sh*te'."

Billy McNeill didn't respect the footballing knowledge of his boss

"Some people I know say he's a very nice man once you get to know him. Everyone is entitled to their opinion I suppose."

Mark Viduka's sarcastic view on Fergus McCann

"He saw me as no different from the groundsman or the head chef."

Lou Macari also wasn't a fan of McCann

"My initial impression of Fergus was that he was a nasty wee chap, and I think I had a good reason."

Andy Walker concurs!

"I told Paul Lambert to aim for the director of football job as it's the best job going. Because you get to sign the players and if they don't do well, then you blame the manager. I think I am angling for that type of job when I get booted out of here. I don't know what it means, but I am going for it."

Martin O'Neill offers sound advice

"The old board were all a*seholes! The deal was done on a Holiday Inn napkin. I should have realised something was wrong as I was in the f*cking Hilton!"

Frank McAvennie

"Being manager is hard enough without going on the board and having to decide whether to sack myself or not."
Martin O'Neill turned down a director's role at Celtic Park

"You pledge your £100,000, get yourself a mobile phone and you're off, you're a football agent."
Fergus McCann

"What was it Nixon said? You guys won't have me to kick around anymore."
Fergus McCann greets the media towards the end of his reign

"I probably did 15 or 20 years as a manager in those three years."

Tommy Burns on chairman Fergus McCann

"There is no one in football I have ever found more difficult to work with."

Wim Jansen on his relationship with general manager Jock Brown

"He has no right whatsoever to form a view of me except from the direct dealings we have had. He never wanted to find out anything about me and has no right to have an opinion on what I am like and what I do."

Jock Brown hits back at Wim Jansen

A FUNNY OLD GAME

"The feeling I got after the goal against Barcelona was just unbelievable! I've never felt anything like that in my life. It was better than sex. We didn't celebrate the win in any particular way. I drank an orange juice, that was quite enough."

Victor Wanyama after scoring in the 2-1 win over Barcelona

"Rangers fans were friendly to me. The most hostility I got was being pelted with snowballs when I went to take a corner at Aberdeen."

Stiliyan Petrov

"I wish I had a f*cking revolver."

Davie Hamilton referring to the referee after getting sent off against Hibernian

"It was not as if it was a broken leg."

Sean Fallon continues playing against Hearts despite cracking his collar bone

"Tell me another career where sleeping for two hours in the afternoon is part of the job? A job where you can act as 17 years old, even though you are 32 and everyone accepts it."

John Colquhoun

"Davie Provan was running rings round Alex McDonald. After one of his runs, he walked past wee Doddy and said, 'I could keep a beach ball away from you in a phone box!'"

Peter Grant on a funny moment against Rangers

"As a footballer learning English, you first learn to swear, then the basic phrases that you need on the pitch."

Henrik Larsson

"Celtic played too much football for my game."

The Bhoys were not direct enough for big Tony Cascarino

"I think a lot of people turned up because they wanted to see what people from Albania looked like."

Murdo MacLeod after 51,000 fans watched Celtic play Partizani Tirana of Communist Albania in a 1979 European Cup tie

"My league debut for Celtic was in October 1969 when we played Raith Rovers. Bobby Murdoch was sitting beside me and asked if I was nervous. 'No' I replied. 'Well' he said, 'You are putting your boots on the wrong feet'. I looked down and he was right."

Kenny Dalglish

"My ears catch so much wind they cost me a yard in speed!"
Peter Wilson, who was regarded as having large ears

TV reporter: "Chris, just what is it that has made Celtic champions this year?"
Chris Sutton: "We got more points than anyone else."

"So I said to myself 'F*ck him, I'm signing'."
Roy Keane after claiming Celtic manager Gordon Strachan said he wasn't worried if he joined or not

"Sometimes you feel that someone is tugging your shirt and you take a quick look at where the linesman is and then you hit the opponent on the hands or in the stomach. Sometimes you get in front of the defender and pull his shorts. If you get hold of 'the package', you pull a bit harder."

Henrik Larsson

"We didn't go swapping our jerseys in those days. We only had two sets of jerseys – one set would be getting cleaned and we would be wearing the other set."

Bobby Carroll couldn't swap shirts with Real Madrid's Ferenc Puskas in 1962

"After the match against Inverness Caley, I felt I was caught up in the Kosovo war, not a damaging football result. Some so-called fans covered my car in spit and shouted obscenities at me... It was Stone Age stuff from reptiles."

Ian Wright after Celtic's 3-2 defeat

"I was in the Celtic team when we won the Scottish Cup and League Championship in 1954. If you never saw us play in those days you will have to take my word for it that I was the best player in the team."

Charlie Tully is very modest

"Coming from Glasgow, the first thing you do if someone kicks you is that you kick them back. This turning the other cheek is a lot of crap."

Paddy Crerand

"Before a game, I always tell myself that it will hurt and it should hurt. I know I am bloody strong, stronger than them. Even if it hurts, it is going to hurt them even more."

Henrik Larsson

"When I first signed I was a cocky little pr*ck."

Scott Brown says he was immature

"I think a success would be to win as many wins as possible and hopefully go on a winning run and win the Scottish Cup."

Interim coach Johan Mjallby wants to win

"£7,000 may be good for a homeless person, but £7,000 a week is not good enough for a top-class international forward."

Pierre van Hooijdonk takes a swipe at the club in a radio interview

"He is one of the most beautiful men you can come across."

Brendan Rodgers fancies Luis Suarez

"Buzzing to be brought all the way up to Inverness with the team to sit in the stands today. Lovely weather for it too."

Anthony Stokes sarcastically tweets after being left out of Celtic's win at Inverness

"Who gives a f*ck about wages when you're not playing! It's about playing and contributing, not picking up a wage."

He followed that up with another outburst

"In Glasgow, half the football fans hate you and the other half think they own you."

Midfielder Tommy Burns

"It was the most wonderfullest feeling in my life."

Jimmy Johnstone reaches high for the superlative when describing the 1967 European Cup win

"We were on £65 a week when I played and I always say that if I was on £25,000 a week they could put boxes of tomatoes around the track and they could throw them at me if I had a bad game. That's the way I see it."

Ex-Celtic player George Connelly on the modern-day footballer

"We played sh*t in the first game in Glasgow and wanted to show that we were the better side tonight."

Henrik Larsson after Celtic's 2-0 second leg win over Blackburn in the UEFA Cup

"My wife Lorraine forced me to go to the doctor, who diagnosed a businessman's ulcer. The doctor asked if I worried about things. I said, 'Well I play for Celtic'."

Peter Grant who was on a month-to-month contract

"I can remember taking my seat in the stand at Hampden before a Scotland game and being picked out by a spectator who was obviously not a Celtic supporter. 'McGrain, ya Fenian b*stard!' he shouted up at me before realising that was not accurate. He then shouted, 'Ya diabetic b*stard!'. I had to laugh."

Danny McGrain who was a diabetic

"Someone threw a pie at me and I was going to eat it but it fell out of my hands. That's probably just as well because the gaffer wouldn't have liked it – there' s too many carbs in it."

Scott Brown after an Aberdeen fan chucked a pie at him following his goal

A Funny Old Game

"Being a goalkeeper is like being the guy in the military who makes the bombs – one mistake and 'bang', everyone gets blown up!"

Artur Boruc

"We were playing Dundalk in Ireland... We left our hotel to drive to the game with two police escorts. In typical Irish tradition, they drove behind the bus."

Davie Provan

"I've been likened to Gerd Muller, Michael Owen and even Lubo Moravcik, but I want to be Shaun Maloney."

Says Shaun Maloney

"The level of goalkeeper coaching at Celtic is much lower than with Legia. I have to obey their orders and as a result I'm getting fat. It's very poor but what can I do?"

Artur Boruc

"I did not go to Manchester United because I didn't fancy their manager Ron Atkinson when I met him. He was too flash. I think he talked more about himself than he did about United. And he could not tell me what position I would play in."

Charlie Nicholas on how he ended up at Arsenal

"If you put that wee thing out on the park, you'll be done for manslaughter."

Jimmy Quinn to manager Willie Maley after seeing the diminutive Patsy Gallacher

"Things are flying at you from different angles – the Buckfast bottle was funny to be fair!"

Leigh Griffiths on objects being thrown at him by Linfield fans

"They have to remember that morality is not suspended because Celtic are in a cup final."

The Archbishop of Glasgow warns Celtic fans to avoid "reckless sexual behaviour" while in Seville for the UEFA Cup final

"There's no comparison between Legia and Celtic supporters. I would give a lot to see 50,000 Legia fans in Celtic's stadium. During the game I feel like I'm in the theatre or cinema. People come to the stadium and pick their nose."

Artur Boruc at a Q&A with former club Legia Warsaw

"I can offer a service at full back – I did it sometimes with Liverpool – but I'm not always at my best there. I think it's a bit like Picasso painting with his left hand: he can do it, but it's not the same picture."

Stephane Henchoz

"I had two negative experiences in my life wearing the No.7 shirt. The first one was with Atletico Madrid and then also with Celtic. But I didn't have any other option. I have played in and always liked the No.10, and if I had that, I would have played better."

Juninho gets the excuses out for his performances at Celtic

"My dad has no interest in football. He used to come and see me play when I was six or seven but he hasn't got a clue. He still watches me, but he thinks I am a centre forward or something."

Midfielder Willo Flood

"I spent some time in Australia and there my friends called me David as it's difficult for some to pronounce my name. If that helps make it easier, it's fine with me."

New signing Ki Sung Yueng

"I scored 180 goals last season."

Winger Frank Brogan also counted his goals in training in a little book

"I don't think that it's a good idea to make friends with people in football. There is no deep relationship between football players."

Artur Boruc doesn't hang around after training

"It's not been easy for me, I no longer have my son [after a custody battle], I've lost my mother and I have broken up with my wife, but I've never been the kind of person to seek excuses."

Stephane Mahe was sent off against Rangers and... finds excuses!

"My only worry is that he's playing with my inheritance money. When he goes, I get it, so he had better be careful."

Paul Dalglish worries about father Kenny's ambitions to buy Celtic

"Scottish women? They are not very pretty."

Artur Boruc

THE FUNNIEST CELTIC QUOTES... EVER!

MANAGING PLAYERS

"After training, he used to remove [his socks] in a car in the car park. I found out and fined him a fiver and I told him it was a fiver every time I found out."

Billy McNeill got annoyed at Charlie Nicholas refusing to wear socks

"He is our player. He definitely has attributes. But he is the sort of player that could get me the sack."

Neil Lennon on Georgios Samaras

"The blond Cafu."

Brendan Rodgers' interesting assessment on Stuart Armstrong

"Is it OK if I give him a skelp if he steps out of line?"

Jock Stein to Billy McNeill's mum when he joined – and she agreed!

"Someone said to me after the match, 'Will you drop him for the next game?'. I was laughing but realised he was serious and then he actually said, 'Are you going to take sanctions?' I didn't know he was a country or was president of Iran. Now we have to stop food parcels getting through to his house! There won't be any sanctions against Artur."

Gordon Strachan after a disappointing performance by Artur Boruc

"He was asked to do a photograph for supporters and he said 'no'. We explained it is part of being a Celtic player and our duty to the fans. He said, 'I don't care'. Then he twice refused to warm up. How long can you put up with someone's arrogance?"

Tommy Burns on Pierre van Hooijdonk

"Scott McDonald, the most intelligent man in the world, Stephen Hawkings him. He knows everything. Every time you tell him something, he knows it, done it, seen it, been it, that's why we call him Stephen Hawkings. That man can do anything!"

Gordon Strachan on Scott McDonald

"If he had a different name – a more Latino name – this guy would be talked about as being worth 15 million quid, for sure."

Brendan Rodgers on 'Senor' Leigh Griffiths

"He has improved so much as a player, maybe because he has cut off his dreadlocks. He is more aerodynamic."

Wim Jansen on Henrik Larsson

"Stewart Kerr? He played about 15 times for Celtic, then discovered crisps when he was 18."

Martin O'Neill on the goalkeeper

"Jimmy is not a bad boy or against authority, but it just seems that if there is trouble or a problem, he is always in the thick of it."

Jock Stein on Jimmy Johnstone

"Chris [Sutton] doesn't like anyone's company. So if he likes [Craig] Bellamy that is a major plus. If he passes the Sutton test, then he should pass anything."

Martin O'Neill

"The fans like to see Bobo Balde wear his shirt on his sleeve."

Kenny Dalglish... erm!

"Charlie Tulley was a journalist's dream – he always had something to say. The story goes that he went to see the film Bonnie Prince Charlie premiere in Glasgow, but he stormed out when it was not about him!"
Bill McNeill

"We will just carry on, the wee b*stard never listens to me anyway."
Jock Stein to the players after Jimmy Johnstone asks to be excused from a team talk to go to the toilet

Jock Stein: "Answer them by scoring."
Paul Wilson: "How about if I score two?"

"He can be a miserable sod when he's not playing. He's like the Grim Reaper walking about the ground, so it's nice to see him back playing."

Gordon Strachan on Craig Beattie

"You and I are alike, I can do everything you can do and I'm 48."

Martin O'Neill on Rafael Scheidt

"Whatever I say, I feel like I'm the Commandant in The Great Escape and you're Steve McQueen. You're always trying to escape, but I'm always trying to bring you back!"

Gordon Strachan on handling Artur Boruc

Billy McNeill: "Will you kick a door to prove you are fit to play?"

David Moyes: "No problem. Which door do you want me to kick?"

The young Moyes was recovering from injury

"We send Bobby Murdoch down to the health farm at Tring to lose some weight and the main result is that we are polluted with bad tips from the wee jockeys he meets there."

Jock Stein

"A 35-year deal if I can manage it."

Martin O'Neill would like Liam Miller to sign until the grand age of 57

THE FUNNIEST CELTIC QUOTES... EVER!

LIFESTYLE CHOICE

"Neilly Mochan was a greyhound enthusiast. I remember he wanted a dog from Ireland and I put him in touch with an owner I knew. Neilly bought it for £80. A few days later, it dropped dead! He never forgave me."

Charlie Tully

"It's embarrassing, I'm not proud of it. I can't even make myself anything to eat. I had to phone her and she said, 'I've left something to put in the microwave'. An hour later and I'm asking, 'Where's the microwave?'"

Gordon Strachan on cooking

Lifestyle Choice

"I am starting to think about life a bit more now. Rather than have an early Chinese for breakfast, I will have a bowl of Corn Flakes."
John Hartson

"I'd dearly love to have played lead guitar with Jethro Tull. That would have done me."
Martin O'Neill

"Shunsuke [Nakamura] told me not to touch alcohol and chips. That was his advice to me – but I tried them one night and I won't be doing that again. I didn't feel too great."
Japanese midfielder Koki Mizuno

"Sven's a lucky man with the ladies. In fact, he's very lucky because, with respect, he's no Brad Pitt."

Martin O'Neill on the England manager

"People say he lived life to the full on and off the pitch. Unfortunately, I lived life to the full with him just one day. We went out drinking in Dundee and my liver is still recovering. My wife didn't speak to me for a week, but it was great fun."

Gordon Strachan on Jimmy Johnstone

"Sex was my pre-match training."

Frank McAvennie

"We all got drunk, I think. For a week after it, we just got drunk."
Jimmy Johnstone on the Lisbon Lions' celebrations

"Just as well you've not got a touch like Bobo Balde or you'd go straight through that window."
Gordon Strachan to motor neurone disease patient Jimmy Johnstone after he controlled his wheelchair with his foot

"It was not until I saw myself on TV that I realised how stupid I looked."
Jonathan Gould after dying his hair blond

"He used to nick my bacon sandwiches. I was always hungry and I was always eating garbage. He used to hijack my food. He would sit down near the bar of our hotel and watch for room service coming. He'd ask the waiter, 'Where are they going? Mr Strachan ordered them, sir? No son, they're for me now'. I used to ring up and say, 'Where's my sandwiches?'. They'd say, 'Mr Stein had them'."

Gordon Strachan on then-Scotland boss Jock Stein

"Is there room in a Ferrari for a child seat? No!"

Logan Bailly insists his 'wild days' are behind him

"After you've signed at Celtic, the first thing you're told is where it's best not to go to refuel your car!"

Jan Vennegoor of Hesselink

"I was not addicted to coke. I was addicted to the lifestyle."

Frank McAvennie

"You go down that pit shaft, a mile underground. You can't see a thing. The guy next to you, you don't know who he is. Yet he is the best friend you will ever have."

Jock Stein on coal miners

"At least they are still eating properly – taking their bananas and proteins. Total professionals."
Gordon Strachan after Jiri Jarosik was pictured in a tabloid holding a banana in a seductive manner

"Davie Provan had these tight jeans and loved wearing four-inch heels because he wanted to look taller."
George McCluskey

"It's not religion that's the problem – it's the lack of religion!"
Jock Stein

"I have already warned him of the dangers of going out in Glasgow. I told him to go down to the Louden Tavern for a couple of nights."

Neil Lennon tries to get Craig Bellamy to visit the Rangers pub

"It was his weekend off. He can do what he wants. Do you spend time with your girlfriend? Do you go to the cinema with her? Would you like her to kiss you now and then? That's what Artur [Boruc] has done. I still go to the cinema with my wife and still kiss her. She doesn't like it, but there you go."

Gordon Strachan after his goalkeeper was spotted in town

"Pat Bonner once came in with this horrendous coat on to training. It was so bad, we hung it from a flagpole above the Jungle."

Roy Aitken

"After I was transferred to Celtic I was walking down Sauchiehall Street when someone shouted, 'You are a big Fenian b*stard!" I had to go home and look up what it meant."

English-born Mick McCarthy

"Going out drinking doesn't help team spirit. When you drink, you just tell lies and talk rubbish."

Gordon Strachan

Lifestyle Choice

"I was out in a bar with a page 3 girl this one time, short skirt and big boobs, the usual. Anyway, this fight broke out and there was beer and glass going everywhere. Frankie Miller, the Scottish singer, was with us but instead of protecting the girl, he dived on top of me to make sure I didn't get hurt! She wasn't best pleased."
Frank McAvennie

"It is such a great advantage to any footballer to have an understanding wife. One who tolerates moods of depression when things are going bad and who somehow always says the right thing at the right time. My wife was perfect."
Charlie Tully

"He once almost got me barred from my golf club. He decided to change his trousers in the car park in front of a few members. They were not impressed!"

Craig Burley on Marc Rieper

"After a game, Italian footballers like to relax with a few glasses of wine. Scottish players prefer a bevy and a shag."

Jim Duffy

"I was brought up in a house that supported Rangers and voted Labour. I signed for Celtic and voted for Maggie [Thatcher] three times."

Davie Provan

"It is always fun getting attacked – one of the highlights of my career. He got fined £100 for that but they got a whip-round in the pub and he got £200."

Gordon Strachan after being assaulted by a Celtic fan as an Aberdeen player

"They say I was nearly a goner. But all I can recollect is seeing a flower box. I could see all these flowers with the different colours, all bright and kind of waving in the wind. Maybe I was passing over to the other side. I don't know why. Is that like being close to death?"

Jock Stein on how he felt after his road accident

"We even competed for the acne cream when we were younger. Obviously I won that one!"

Gordon Strachan on former Aberdeen teammate Alex McLeish

"When I first broke into the Celtic team, my pre-match meal was cooked by my father in our house in Maryhill. I never had steak or pasta – I had three hot dogs."

Charlie Nicholas

"Your hospitality, your Guinness and your girls were unbelievable."

Jock Stein praises his Irish hosts after a pre-season tour of Ireland

"Listen, if I had a pound for every girl I could remember being with, I'd be a millionaire."
Frank McAvennie when a girl in a night club asked if he remembered her

Q: "What would you have done if you hadn't been a footballer?"
A: "A funeral director. I like looking at dead bodies."
Chris Sutton

'

"I have no doubt that the things I learn in my taekwondo class will enhance my goalkeeping career."
Magnus Hedman

BEST OF ENEMIES

Interviewer: "What about Rangers getting to the UEFA Cup Final?"

Gordon Strachan: "I have no problem, we couldn't get the chance to beat them. We weren't in their competition!"

"I am not going to answer any more questions on Rangers because they are not on our radar."

Neil Lennon

"I certainly didn't need a lip-reader to work out what 30,000 were calling me."

Neil Lennon after Rangers had claimed that a lip-reader said he made offensive comments to their fans

"I felt the burning hostility, especially when a pie hit me on the chest."

Tony Cascarino on an away Old Firm game

"I remember Jock telling reporters he had two 15-year-olds he wanted to sign. He said one was a Catholic and one a Protestant and he was going to sign the Protestant first. They asked why. He said, 'Because I know Rangers will not sign a Catholic'."

Bertie Auld

"Rangers are alright, but they still haven't invented blue grass."

Jock Stein

"The Old Firm match is the only one in the world where the managers have to calm the interviewers down."

Tommy Burns

"I might even agree to become Rangers' first Catholic if they paid me £1m and bought me Stirling Castle. Let me spell out where I stand. I am a Celtic man through and through and so I dislike Rangers because they are a force in Scottish football and therefore a threat to the club I love. But more than that, I hate the religious policy they maintain."

Maurice Johnstone – a year before signing for Rangers

"I've always seen us as the Cavaliers and them as the Roundheads."

Billy McNeill compares Celtic with Rangers

"I'm not even liked in my own household, so I'll be fine."

Martin O'Neill on the prospect of facing flak from Rangers supporters

Rangers fan: "You only won the European Cup because you had five Protestants in your team."

Jock Stein: "Well you've never won it and you've got 11."

"He is not a bad lad. If he said, 'God bless Myra Hindley', I might have a problem."
Gordon Strachan after keeper Artur Boruc wound up the Rangers fans by wearing a 'God Bless the Pope' t-shirt

"I've never heard the second verse of the Sash as we have usually scored by then."
Roy Aitken

"Why should I shake hands with any player? I don't like them, I don't like the club and I don't like the players – end of story. I don't have to love anyone."
'Holy Goalie' Artur Boruc on Rangers

"I'm often asked how this Rangers team compares with the Lisbon Lions. I have to be honest and say I think it would be a draw but, then, some of us are getting on for 60."

Bertie Auld on Rangers reaching the Champions League group stages for the first time

"Next time we play, please do not call me 'that wee humphy b*stard'."

Patsy Gallacher jokes with the Rangers chairman Sir John Ure Primrose after playing for Rangers in a benefit game for their striker Andy Cunningham

"It was like Goldilocks and the Three Bears."

Frank McAvennie on being sent off in an Old Firm clash, along with Rangers trio Graham Roberts, Terry Butcher and Chris Wood

"The only time I know is seven past Niven."

Charlie Tully when asked the time by a fan after Celtic beat Rangers 7-1 – George Niven was the Rangers keeper

"For a while, I did unite Rangers and Celtic fans. There were people in both camps that hated me."

Maurice Johnstone

"I might start panicking tonight, take a drink and become an alcoholic. But the TV is alright tonight, so we should be OK."

Gordon Strachan when asked about the threat of Rangers

"Sometimes you get the odd 'f*ck off' but mostly it's tongue in cheek. They might want to take a picture, do a film, posing as Celtic fans then saying something Rangers. I might then say '5-1', and then walk away laughing."

Mikael Lustig on meeting Rangers fans

"Old firm games are all right, as long as you win."

Kenny Dalglish

THE FUNNIEST CELTIC QUOTES... EVER!

TALKING BALLS

John Thomson: "One of their players called me a papist b*stard!"

Jimmy McGrory: "Don't worry, I've been called that hundreds of times."

John Thomson: "But you are one!"

Thomson was a non-Catholic

"You know why he was so good on his right side? It was because he kept his teeth in his bunnet down there in the corner of the net!"

Jimmy Johnstone on goalie Ronnie Simpson

"We're slightly different characters – he reads and I cannae."

Scott Brown on Stuart Armstrong

"Quite frankly he was a dirty wee b*stard."
Tommy Gemmell on Bertie Auld

"Touch like an angel... Jesus f****** Christ. Do a normal interview, get in changing room and celebrate. #billybigtime."
Leigh Griffiths tweets about Hibs star Jason Cummings who said he showed "the touch of an angel" after scoring twice against Rangers

"Paul is so good he could play in his shirt and tie."
Rab Douglas on Paul Lambert

"John Hartson is the laziest player I've seen. When you look at him you can easily see he needs some exercise."

Celtic goalkeeper Artur Boruc

"Speak to me when you are better dressed!"

A fearless John Gilchrist to manager Willie Maley after a dressing-room row

"I was terrified of Jock Stein. He even frowned on Coca-Cola. If he spotted you sneaking a Coke to your room at night, he'd throw it down the sink and say, 'I'll Coca-Cola you!'"

Lou Macari

"Greigy hit me once. I got up and then a moment later I was down again. Then seconds after that, he dumped me on the track at Ibrox. I said to him, 'John, are you trying to intimidate me?'"

Jimmy Johnstone on Rangers defender John Greig

Willie Maley to his wing halves: "Carry the ball forward."

Tommy McInally: "Is that not a foul."

Willie Maley: "What is?"

Tommy McInally: "Carrying the ball, using your hands."

"Bobby Lennox had a lucky suit and was superstitious about not wearing it in case we got beat. By the end you could almost see your face in the arse of his trousers."

Jimmy Johnstone

"When Billy McNeill was recovering from a heart operation, I called to see how he was and his eight-year-old grandson James picked up the phone. He asked who I was and when I told him, he snapped back, 'You're the guy that gave away the penalty in Lisbon!'."

Jim Craig

"Billy [McNeill] sets a high standard of conduct for all of us and this is the main reason why you do not see any long-haired wonders walking through the doors at Celtic Park... Professional football is our business. We feel we do not have to look like a crowd of discotheque drop-outs to attract attention."

Bobby Murdoch

"He told me that training started at 10.30am when it was really 10am. He was trying to get me fined on my first day!"

New signing Steve Guppy was almost stitched up by his pal Neil Lennon

"He's a moaning t*at, let's put it that way, but that's what makes him a winner."

Garry Parker on Neil Lennon

"My most embarrassing moment was trying to follow Craig Burley's instructions in a Celtic game when he didn't have his teeth in and getting it hopelessly wrong."

Malky Mackay

"He could scare the sh*t out of you."

John Fallon on Jock Stein

"Ally McCoist is like dogsh*t in the penalty area. You don't know he's there until the damage is done."

John Hughes

"Jimmy did not like flying. He used to carry a bottle of holy water on our flights."

Bobby Lennox on Jimmy Johnstone

"They did not lace up Jimmy's boots before a game, they laced up his head and put him on the park."

Tommy McInally on Jimmy McGrory

"I don't want to put pressure on him, but I don't think I've ever seen anything like him."

Alan Thompson is not exactly keeping the pressure off teammate Aiden McGeady

"It's not because Regi's crap, it's just cockney rhyming slang. Regi Blinker – stinker."

Ian Wright explains why he told new his teammate that he "had a Regi" at training

"I've seen many players like him – he just behaves like a star."

Artur Boruc doesn't rate Roy Keane

"Don, here is a complimentary ticket. Would you not be better watching me from up there in the stand?"

Charlie Tulley to Aberdeen defender Don Emery

"It was amazing to see thousands of fans outside the stadium the night [Robbie] Keane signed. I think only one guy turned up for me."

Poor old Glenn Loovens

"He's like a dog on the pitch."

Stiliyan Petrov on Neil Lennon

THE FUNNIEST CELTIC QUOTES... EVER!

CAN YOU MANAGE?

"People don't understand a manager wanting to spend more time with his wife and family. Do I wait until people are screaming at me, my wife is going off her head and I'm a nervous wreck? I love football, but it's not an obsession."

Unemployed Gordon Strachan, shortly before his Celtic arrival

"I will calm down when I retire or die."

Martin O'Neill refers to his animated style on the touchline

"Celtic jerseys are not for second-best, they don't shrink to fit inferior players."

Jock Stein

Can You Manage?

"Never fall in love with them, because they'll two-time you."

Jock Stein's advice on players to Alex Ferguson

"When I was at Celtic, I was said to be a players' man and maybe that was true. In those days, if the ship was sinking I would have thrown all 11 lifebelts to the players. Now I would keep one for myself, throw them and lose a player."

David Hay

"My best-ever signing was my wife, Marina."

Kenny Dalglish

"I've heard it said that you can't be a football manager and tell the truth. Well, I'm going to have a go at it."

Liam Brady after becoming Celtic boss

"Go out and enjoy yourself. It will be the last time that you wear a Celtic jersey."

Jock Stein to an unnamed player at half-time during a reserve game

"The world looks a totally different place after two wins. I can even enjoy watching Blind Date or laugh at Noel's House Party."

Gordon Strachan

Can You Manage?

"I don't believe everything Bill tells me about his players. If they had been that good, they'd not only have won the European Cup, but the Ryder Cup, the Boat Race and even the Grand National!"

Jock Stein on Liverpool manager Bill Shankly

"As a manager you either walk on water – or you're the devil."

Brendan Rodgers

"Some people will say it's madness for me to take this job. I'm ready to invest in madness."

Martin O'Neill on joining Celtic

"Anybody who is thinking of applying for the Scotland job in the next eight or nine years should go get themselves checked out by about 15 psychiatrists."

Martin O'Neill on Scotland manager Berti Vogts

"Just like 17 per cent of us have ginger hair, a lot of us Scots are small. You could build up a hugely talented Celtic side and Snow White would have to lead them out because there are so many small people here."

Gordon Strachan

"There should be a law against him. He knows what's happening 20 minutes before anyone else."

Jock Stein on Bobby Moore

"You have to get used to the pressure. There is no release unless you are a Buddhist monk and you meditate, they tell me that works well. I've got a local pub I go to on a Saturday night at about 9.30pm. Everybody there is not interested in football. You go and talk about who is doing what in the village."

Gordon Strachan likes to escape the goldfish bowl

"The secret of being a good manager is to keep the six players who hate you away from the five who are undecided."

Jock Stein

"Time was when the budget at Celtic was the fourth or fifth biggest in British football. Nowadays we're finding we can't compete for wages with the likes of Hull City!"

Gordon Strachan

"Players are not puppets. You don't sit in a dugout and pull strings to make them jump."

Jock Stein

Can You Manage?

"This is no use to me because I don't drink coffee. Where I come from in the Muirhouse district in Edinburgh, no one was brought up to drink coffee."

Manager Gordon Strachan panics after Celtic's supply of tea bags was confiscated by US customs on their pre-season tour

"At Celtic, you're a draw away from a crisis."

Paul Lambert

"We must not be too clever, we must only be clever."

Jock Stein

"Old Firm supporters went to internationals to cheer three players, boo two, and ignore the rest!"

Jock Stein on Scotland fans

"We do have the greatest fans in the world, but I've never seen a fan score a goal."

Jock Stein puts things into perspective

"If form was the only factor we would all win the pools every week."

Jock Stein

Can You Manage?

"[Other managers] are seen as a breath of fresh air for calling things as they see them, whereas I'm perceived as the enfant terrible or the thug on the touchline."
Neil Lennon

"If you can manage Celtic, you can be prime minister."
Gordon Strachan

"It's not my job to keep everyone happy. I'm not a social worker."
Martin O'Neill

THE FUNNIEST CELTIC QUOTES... EVER!

MEDIA CIRCUS

"The media coverage for Tommy [Burns] over the last few days has been fantastic, even the half-wit on Real Radio was quite good."
Gordon Strachan has a dig at the local station

"You people sometimes are like those serial killers you see in films who send out these horrible messages. The serial killer who cuts out the words 'I'm going to get you' or 'Your wife is next'. You are the very same."
Gordon Strachan on the Scottish media

Reporter: "Gordon, a clean sheet... it's been a while since you managed to say that?"
Gordon Strachan: "Aye... I was about 15."

"One or two 'voices of football' – I've been told – said that we played 4-5-1. That was terrific to work out because I never worked that out. You must be better geniuses than me. I must be really ordinary because I sent out a 4-4-2.

If you saw something else then that was fantastic. I was wasting my time getting my badges – I should have just joined a radio station."

Gordon Strachan in buoyant mood with the press after winning the League Cup

"If they were interested in what I had to say they would get here in time. The door stays shut!"

Jock Stein doesn't allow late journalists to attend his press conferences

Journalist: "But what of the done deal at Rangers that was alleged by various radio stations?"

Scott Brown: "It just shows you radio stations talk just as much crap as you do. Everyone was saying I had signed for Rangers when I was sitting in my house."

The new signing puts the record straight at the media conference

"Fans can be easily manipulated by you. You can start wars you people, never mind going for managers."

Gordon Strachan takes aim at the reporters

Gary Lineker: "So Gordon, if you were English, what formation would you play?"

Gordon Strachan: "If I was English, I'd top myself."

The Celtic manager as a 2006 World Cup TV pundit

Journalist: "Is there any other club you would have left Leicester for?"

Martin O'Neill: "There is one, but the best manager in the world is there and he isn't giving up yet."

Exchange at the manager's first Celtic press conference

"You talk about that question but that shouldn't be asked now because I think I've proved that. What you should ask is who is posing the question? Not an intelligent person, that's for sure. It's someone who's sitting with his tracksuit on, his devil dug at his side and a can of Kestrel in his hand, maybe coked up to his eyeballs, shouting down the phone. I'm not answering to that. I'm not answering a question from Mr Ned."

Gordon Strachan's rant at the media when asked about the pressure of Champions League qualifiers

"None of the Celtic players stood up and counted."

Frank McAvennie as a pundit

"If I put Riordan in instead of Nakamura, you're off your head; take Aiden out, you're off your head; leave Maciej out, you're off your head. So basically, I'm off my head."

Gordon Strachan says the media will never be happy with the side he picks

Journalist: "What's it like to go from zero to hero?"

Lubo Moravcik to his interpreter: "Tell him I was never a zero."

"Britain's Got Talent is absolutely fantastic – the funniest thing on TV. I can't wait to get home."

Gordon Strachan

"Since coming to Celtic a few months ago, the newspapers have linked me with 210 players. Fair enough, but some of those mentioned I am not interested in, some I've never heard of and two of them are dead."

Martin O'Neill

"Trying to explain it to you would be impossible. It would be like you trying to explain childbirth to me."

Gordon Strachan to a (childless) female reporter who asked for his view on a defeat by St Mirren

"Really? The boy who played today then was better than Artur Boruc. What a great place this new training academy is. We are cloning players now. Now that we have two, maybe I can sell one and keep the other."

Gordon Strachan after a reporter said he heard that Boruc did not train with the squad

"What sort of state do I leave Celtic in? Certainly a better state than I found them, and certainly a better state than you're in."

Martin O'Neill to the press on departing as Celtic manager

"I just needed a [summer] break. Like I said I don't have a problem with the players speaking, but I'd imagine that most newspaper guys needed a break from me as well!"

Gordon Strachan enjoys his time off during the close season

Reporter: "How does it feel to be back managing where it all began all those years ago?"

Gordon Strachan: "Old."

The manager speaking ahead of a return to his former club Dundee

"The papers say I'm Celtic's first Protestant manager. I prefer to say 25 per cent of our managers have been Protestant."

Jock Stein, Celtic's fourth-ever manager

"Well, not if you and I keep talking about it."

Gordon Strachan when asked if a change of tactics would surprise opponents Spartak

"I know that two miles south of Carlisle, nobody has ever heard of them."

Martin O'Neill has a pop at Scottish football journalists

Printed in Great Britain
by Amazon

29330157R00075